# The Colony of Rhode Island

Susan Whitehurst

The Rosen Publishing Group's
## PowerKids Press™
New York

For Keaton

Published in 2000 by The Rosen Publishing Group, Inc.
29 East 21st Street, New York, NY 10010

Photo Credits: Cover and title page, pp. 1, 4, 7, 8, 11, 12, 16, 19, 20 © Granger Collection; p. 22 © Image Works; p. 15 © Art Resource.

First Edition

Book Design: Andrea Levy

Whitehurst, Susan.
      The Colony of Rhode Island / by Susan Whitehurst.
            p.     cm. — (The library of the thirteen colonies and the Lost Colony)
      Includes index.
      Summary: Traces the history of Rhode Island from the arrival of the first European settlers in the early seventeenth century through 1790 when it became the thirteenth state to join the Union.
      ISBN 0-8239-5476-5
      1. Rhode Island—History—Colonial period, ca. 1600-1775 Juvenile literature.  2. Rhode Island—History—1775-1865 Juvenile literature.  [1. Rhode Island—History—Colonial period, ca. 1600–1775.  2. Rhode Island—History—1775-1865.]   I. Title. II. Series.
      F82.W47 1999
      974.5'02—dc21                                                                     99-26048
                                                                                              CIP

Manufactured in the United States of America

# Contents

# The Colony of Rhode Island

The history of the **colony** of Rhode Island began in England. In the 1600s, the king of England started a new religion that everyone in the country had to join. A group of people called **Puritans** were against the new religion. They

There's a story that says a Dutch sailor saw red clay in Narragansett Bay. He called the land Roodt Eylandt, or red island, in Dutch.

decided to leave England and go to the Massachusetts colony in America. In Massachusetts, anyone who disagreed with the Puritans' religious beliefs was breaking the law. Roger Williams disagreed. Williams thought people should be able to worship as they liked. These ideas would later lead Williams to found the colony of Rhode Island.

◀ *Puritans had very strict rules about how people should dress and act.*

# Williams Leaves Massachusetts

Williams broke the law and spoke out against the Puritans in Massachusetts. In January 1636, the Puritans planned to arrest Williams and send him back to England. Williams left his home and family and headed for Narragansett Bay, to the area that would later become Rhode Island. Williams wanted to begin a new colony where the church and the government would be separate. After days of walking, Williams came to a Wampanoag Indian village. The chief, Massasoit, welcomed Williams to the village. Williams stayed for several months.

Williams published a book about the Indians' languages and customs called *A Key Into the Language of America.*

*Roger Williams was welcomed by the Wampanoag because he had been at the first Thanksgiving.* ▶

# A New Beginning

Williams found other people who wanted to start a new **settlement**. In June 1636, they bought land from the Indians, and built some huts there. Williams named this small town Providence, which means "guided by God."

In the next few years, more **settlers** who disagreed with the Puritans in Massachusetts came to live in and around Providence. They built three more towns: Portsmouth, Newport, and Warwick. In 1643, the four towns decided to join together and become an official English colony. The colonists sent Roger Williams to England to get permission from the king. The king of England approved the colony. He gave the settlers a **charter**, which protected them from being taken over by other colonies or other countries.

◀ *Roger Williams bought land from the Indians in order to begin a new settlement.*

# Growth and Change

Twenty years later, when a new king became the ruler of England, Williams had to return to England for a new charter. The Charter of 1663 said that the people of Rhode Island had full religious freedom. Soon people of many religions, including Quakers, Catholics, and Jews, moved to Rhode Island. The charter also permitted the Rhode Island **colonists** to make many of their own laws and choose their own **governor**. Any man who owned land in Rhode Island could vote. Several men from each town formed the part of the government called the General Assembly.

The first Quaker meetinghouse was built in Newport in 1699. Newport is also the home of the oldest synagogue in the nation.

*The country's first synagogue was built in Newport, Rhode Island.* ▶

# The Indians and the Settlers Fight

Williams always treated the Indians fairly. He studied the Indian language and customs. Many colonists took land from the Indians without paying for it. Williams tried to make sure that settlers paid the Indians for their land. In 1662,

During King Philip's War, Williams asked the Indians to spare Providence. Few people were killed there, but many buildings burned.

Massasoit's son became chief of the Wampanoag. The colonists called him King Philip. King Philip was angry because many colonists had cheated Indians out of their land. He got four other tribes to join him and try to drive the settlers out of New England. The war that followed was called King Philip's War. King Philip died during fighting in Rhode Island in 1676.

*◀ Thousands of people were killed in King Philip's War.*

# Colonial Farms and Businesses

By the year 1700, about 6,000 people lived in Rhode Island. Towns on the coast were very busy. Colonists fished and gathered clams, lobsters, and oysters from Narragansett Bay. They built ships and shipped beef and wool to other colonies and countries. Some colonists hunted whales. Whale oil was used in lamps, and a waxy material from whales made good candles.

Ships from Africa also brought slaves to Rhode Island. One-fifth of all the slaves in the colonies came through Rhode Island. Although the Rhode Island colonists had many good ideas about people's religious and political rights, they had not yet learned to respect the rights of the Africans.

*Whaling ships were a big part of Colonial Rhode Island's industry.* ▶

# England Taxes the Colonists

By the 1700s, Rhode Island and the other colonies were doing so well that England wanted a share of their wealth. England and France had been fighting on and off for control of America for over 74 years. These wars were called the French and Indian Wars. At the end of the wars, England owed a lot of money for all of the soldiers, weapons, and forts that they had used. To raise money, England decided to tax the colonists for sugar, paper, and tea. Many colonists became angry and refused to pay the taxes. England sent soldiers, called redcoats because they wore red jackets, to the colonies to make the colonists pay the taxes.

*Colonists protested England's taxes by tarring and feathering tax collectors.*

# The Colonists Rebel

Rhode Islanders were so angry about the taxes that they burned two English ships called the *Liberty* and the *Gaspee*. Then, in 1774, the colonists sent men to a meeting in Philadelphia called the First Continental Congress. The congress

> The colonists who trained to be soldiers were called minutemen because they could be ready to fight in a minute.

met to decide if the colonies should remain under English rule or join together to form a new nation. The congress asked the king of England, King George III, for fairer treatment. King George III refused. Redcoats marched to Lexington, Massachusetts on April 19, 1775. About 75 colonial soldiers, called **minutemen**, were waiting for them and war broke out!

The *Liberty* and the *Gaspee* were burned because Rhode Islanders did not want to pay taxes to England. ▶

# Fighting the British

On May 4, 1776, Rhode Island was the first colony to say that it would no longer obey King George III or the laws of England. On July 4, 1776, Rhode Island joined the other colonies in approving the Declaration of Independence, which said that the colonies were now their own country.

During the war, George Washington was in charge of the American army and Esek Hopkins, from Rhode Island, was in charge of the navy. The navy only had eight ships, but private ships called **privateers** also fought at sea. While fighting for their freedom, the Rhode Island colonists decided to stop bringing in slaves from Africa. Although this did not end slavery in Rhode Island, it was an important first step toward recognizing that slavery is wrong.

◀ *Esek Hopkins was the head of the navy during the Revolutionary War.*

# Rhode Island's Ideas

   On October 19, 1781, the English surrendered to General George Washington. The colonists had won the war. On May 29, 1790, Rhode Island became the thirteenth state in the United States. Rhode Islanders had lots of ideas about how the nation's new government should work. These early ideas about freedom of religion and freedom of speech are still remembered by the **lawmakers** at work in the Rhode Island State House in today's Providence (above). Rhode Island is a small state with big ideas!

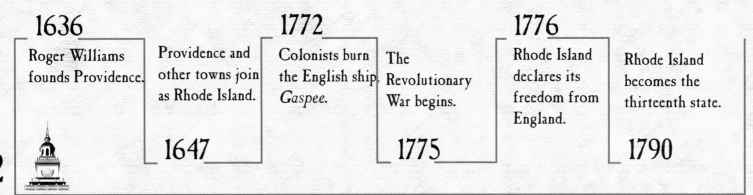

**1636**
Roger Williams founds Providence.

Providence and other towns join as Rhode Island.
**1647**

**1772**
Colonists burn the English ship *Gaspee*.

The Revolutionary War begins.
**1775**

**1776**
Rhode Island declares its freedom from England.

Rhode Island becomes the thirteenth state.
**1790**

# Glossary

**charter** (CHAR-tur)  An official paper giving someone permission to do something.

**colonists** (KAH-luh-nists)  People who live in a colony.

**colony** (KAH-luh-nee)  An area in a new country where a large group of people move, who are still ruled by the leaders and laws of their old country.

**governor** (GUH-vuh-nur)  A political leader in a state.

**lawmakers** (LAW-may-kurz)  People who work in a city, state, or national government and help to make rules, or laws.

**minutemen** (MI-nuht-men)  Colonial American colonists, who were trained to fight, and could be ready in a minute.

**privateers** (pri-vuh-TEERZ)  Privately owned ships (not the navy) that helped fight the Revolutionary War.

**Puritans** (PYUR-ih-tinz)  People in the 1500s and 1600s who belonged to the Protestant religion.

**settlement** (SEH-tuhl-mint)  A new land where people are just beginning to live.

**settler** (SEH-tuh-lur)  A person who moves to a new land to live.

# Index

# Web Sites:

You can learn more about Colonial Rhode Island on the Internet. Check out this Web site:
http://ns.sprintout.com/foodbasket/rhodeisland.html